Personal Life Management:
A Guide to Personal Excellence

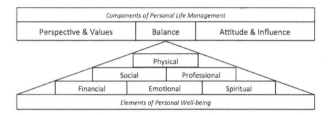

Bruce Flareau, MD

Author of the Six Ps of Physician Leadership

ISBN-13: 978-0-9899981-1-6
ISBN-10: 0-9899981-1-8

Kumu Press
5847 Long Bayou Way
St. Petersburg, FL 33708
727-403-2637
kumupress@gmail.com
www.kumupress.com

Special Orders. Discounts are available on quantity purchases of 10 or more copies. Please contact Kumu Press at the above address.

Table of Contents

Dedication

I want to thank my wife and children for their patience during the writing of this work. Having led many workshops over the years I have used family examples (including pictures) on numerous occasions to make my points. My family is my strength and I dedicate this writing to my wife Kathy and my daughters Danielle and Christine.

What Readers are Saying

"Personal Life Management brings insight into the stresses of living in the 21st century. Dr. Flareau provides practical tools that can guide you to a happier, healthier way of leading your life."

- Terry Bradley, MD

"For those who know Bruce, his book Personal Life Management, A Guide to Self-Actualization is not just a compact, all-encompassing and efficient work on the keys to achieving happiness and success in life. It is absolutely the personal user manual for how he lives his own successful and fulfilling life. I have met many successful people in my life, but few who are as truly enlightened as Bruce Flareau."

- Stewart Schaffer, CEO,
C- Suite Solutions

A few years ago, I attended one of Bruce Flareau's Personal Life Management retreats, politely expecting to have my own personal life management strategies validated. But as the first session began, and Dr. Flareau asked me to imagine myself at my own funeral, listening to my loved ones eulogize me, I realized that this was going to be much more than just an affirmation of my own approach. I was actually going to discover something new about myself! Next came the house on fire exercise, in which I, like so many other participants, I suspect, neglected to include the "people" that mattered to me in my rescue priority list, instead listing only the "things". Embarrassment aids educational retention, it appears, and my face was red indeed as I acknowledged my omission to the group. I can feel a blush beginning now as I recall that moment. But the exercise that impacted me the most that day, and has continued to do so since, was being asked to write down my own personal mission statement. As a budding physician executive, I had pokers in many fires and rarely turned down an invitation to participate in whatever opportunity presented itself, so long as the content seemed concordant with my professional trajectory. I had never before put into writing "why" I had made the choices I made. I had always assumed that everyone would be able to see the purpose behind it all, to infer my intent. But I realized, in that moment, that even I was sometimes unsure of the "why". Crafting a personal mission statement caused me to crystallize my beliefs and life goals into an actionable dictum, which has informed my choices since and facilitated more effective self-advocacy. I am not being hyperbolic when I say that Dr. Flareau's retreat changed my life.

- Stephen A. Leedy, MD MA FAAHPM HMDC, President & CEO, Upstreaming

Preface

Two authors and leaders of people, Tom Stevenin and Steven Covey, have heavily influenced much of this writing. Tom Stevenin, a self-made man who himself said he learned similar things from a cereal box cardboard record. Many reading this work will not remember 45 speed records, nor the cardboard punch-outs that could be played with a needle powered phonograph, but all will identify with a chance phrase, video clip or other work that sparks something inside of them. I met Tom on a few occasions and listened to his teachings and it resonated with me. Tom was a self-made businessman who passed prematurely in life. However, his teachings go on and are a tribute to the man who once described himself to audiences as "little retardo", a nickname given to him by children who were as critical as you would expect them to be. However he used that experience to reinvent himself and to lift himself up and move forward. I am confident that his teachings have helped many and will continue to do so.

Steven Covey, on the other hand is not someone I have met in person but I have read his book the Seven Habits of Highly Effective People on many occasions and consider it a must-read for everyone. I was delighted to know that my daughters had to read it when they were in middle school. It is landmark work that lays the groundwork for writings and activities such as this. Also lost to us now, his son, who I have met, carries on his tradition of teaching.

Finally, over the last 25 years we have had the opportunity to coach many individuals in their personal journeys towards life happiness and self-fulfillment. From my early career days as an academic and practicing family physician and program director to my later years as a physician executive, there have been numerous opportunities to share and to learn from one another. I will share some of these stories, both physician and non-physician related, in the pages that follow.   Oliver Oyama, Jeff Sourbeer and I developed leadership materials for our students, a portion of which was based upon these principles. Later we created local and regional coaching opportunities that put these fundamentals to work over and over again.   We have shaped them and continue to evolve components both to keep the examples relevant and the messages clear. While we have stood on the shoulders of giants, this work is a compilation of all of those interactions, many other readings and writings, and personal life experiences.

Introduction

Personal Life Management: A Guide to Living a Balanced and Fulfilled Life

The Inuit people of the arctic long ago created signs and symbols to aid their fellow man in safe passage in their journeys across unfamiliar lands; they called these symbols Inuksuk. This writing is in many ways our Inukshuk as it is an aid to safe passage in the journey of life. It borrows from many authors on the subject of life management and weaves them together into practical considerations for us all. We have taught these principles for over 25 years and have had wide varieties of emotional reactions from personal breakthroughs of crying and emotional elation to flattened disinterest. There is no perfect recipe for happiness, instead it is an internal journey based upon our own values and priorities. So let this book help you as a personal guide of self-discovery, as a vehicle of discipline to take some time to focus on yourself, your values, your priorities, your dreams and your plans to accomplish them.

Larger than life-sized Inukshuk in Churchill, Canada surrounded by a "sun dog"

- Photo by Bruce Flareau

This writing is broken into three categories of personal life management with the second category, (personal balance) having six subcomponents of its own. Each is explored in its own chapter with examples and practical narrative. The diagram below is a visual reminder of where we will be as we explore these concepts and how they fit together as one. The current section being discussed will be highlighted at the beginning of the chapter in red.

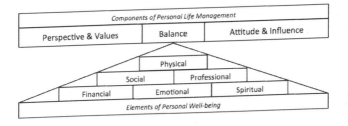

"

"We shall not cease from exploration,
and the end of all our exploring
will be to arrive where we started
and know the place for the first time."

T.S. Eliot

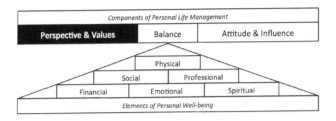

Components of Personal Life Management		
Perspective & Values	Balance	Attitude & Influence

Physical
Social | Professional
Financial | Emotional | Spiritual

Elements of Personal Well-being

Chapter 1: Perspective & Attitude

How you view the world is critical to your happiness. It has been said that life is 20% what happens to you and 80% how you react to it. We will talk more later of the emerging area of positive psychology but let us first take a snapshot of ourselves and how we as individuals view the world or more directly stated, " What is your perspective?" Let us take the example of a day in which you are traveling to an important meeting across town and traffic comes to a standstill. It is a hot day already, your automotive air conditioner is on the fritz, you are running late, and the traffic is backed up beyond description. Suddenly a car from behind takes to the shoulder and begins fighting its way around cars, beeping and edging dangerously close to the cars ahead and alongside. You might come to the conclusion that this is a crazy lunatic who is self-absorbed and thinks their need to move ahead is greater than your own. You might become angry, or even yell in your vehicle. Your reaction is based upon limited facts but is in fact your perception of what is happening. You assign some value to that based upon learned beliefs and you perhaps react emotionally, all based upon your own perspective of the world. But what if you were to learn that the driver had just received word that their daughter was in a life threatening accident and had been air lifted to an area hospital and was not expected to live out the hour. Would your perspective change? As a result of changing your perspective would your mood change, your degree of compassion, the tenure of your attitude, the tone of your day? For most people the answer would be yes.

So how you view the world in fact impacts your degree of happiness or lack thereof, in the moment. Perspective, and the self-realization that you have a perspective, is perhaps the first place in which to begin to change yourself in the progression of being a happier and more self-actualized person.

Remember that to be alive is to have problems. At some point we will all be faced with unexpected situations and problems. In fact, some would argue that the more successful you are, the more problems you encounter and thus problems are the byproduct of success, however you may measure that. So if problems and difficulties are inherent and your response is within your control, it would seem reasonable to develop conscious ways in which to manage your response or your perspective.

Taking this notion of perspective to the extreme let us use some classic Steven Covey teachings to begin with the end in mind. The ultimate end would be your own death. Steven tells us to imagine ourselves at our own funeral with loved ones, co-workers, or others giving the eulogy. What would they say? Would their view of us align with our self-perception? Is our perspective of ourselves distorted? We each see ourselves through our own minds eyes and hence it would be no surprise that others would see us somewhat different than we see ourselves. However if the gap is large, perhaps it is our self-image that is disparate and may be the best place to begin. For example, if while sitting at your own funeral, you are expecting to hear your spouse or child speak of you as a loving and dedicated husband or father, are you certain this is what they see and/or will say? Do you forget the birthdays, the graduations, and the special moments? Are you too caught up in yourself or work? Do you spend enough time with family? Have you earned that eulogy or is that just your misperception? Taking time to write your own eulogy through the eyes of others is a difficult task if taken seriously. It is even harder to validate those writings with those loved ones in the attempt of making course corrections while you are alive to do so. Peter Drucker, the great management guru was quoted as telling followers to spend their time on what was important rather than what was urgent. To do this effectively would mean that you have taken the time, energy and focus to determine what is important to you. Perhaps a good use of time for us all.

During seminars we have heard participants tell us that the opinions of others are not important. That the eulogy exercise is more about the readers than it is about themselves; we mostly disagree. It is a reality check to assist us in aligning who we are with what we want to be. Alfred Nobel was a Swedish chemist, innovator and the inventor of dynamite amongst holding patents on some 350 other inventions. One day his obituary was erroneously published before his death and it spoke of his legacy efforts in developing dynamite. Upon reading this he realized this was not how he wanted others to see him – it was "ego dystonic". That is to say, it made him feel unaligned with how he wanted to feel. And so he created the Nobel Peace prize!

Taking stock of yourself or more accurately how you perceive the world and yourself in it is the first step in personal life management. Not with the intent of controlling how others think but rather of validating and aligning who you believe yourself to be. Practically speaking, if you begin to see the splendor and wonder of the world, your overall demeanor might change.

A friend once told me about a car he saw cruising his neighborhood on various occasions. He was concerned that the driver was up to no good and was casing the neighborhood to commit a future robbery. He later found out that the car was driven by a teenage boy who was learning to drive and was practicing by driving about the neighborhood as often as he was allowed and able. Why did my friend jump to the darker conclusion? Perhaps his disposition, in matters of personal protection and security was to assume the worst. This is a small example but imagine that perspective magnified across everything you see and experience. I am not advocating for blind naiveté either, but simply a heightened sense of self-awareness and a willingness to change.

Attitude, like perspective, is very much an inward facing manifestation of how your mind is programmed to respond to the world about you. Do you see the glass half empty or half full? Do you have a negative response to goings on or a positive response? Psychologists today speak of positive psychology, which is a way in which to reprogram your mind to see the good in the world. Renowned psychologist Martin Seligman and others founded this specific area of study at the turn of the millennium. It explores the ideas about what leads to personal well-being and happiness.

This emerging field of study broadens our understanding of psychology in which we often focus upon emotional weakness or pathology, to one instead that is equally about the concepts of emotional strength and virtue; not just fixing what is broken but nurturing what is best. A colleague of mine showed me a quote from an unknown source that said "Psychotherapy makes miserable people less miserable, but not happy. Positive psychology makes ordinary people much happier." I am not a psychologist, but there seems to be something to that. In 4th century BC

Aristotle is quoted as saying that "happiness is the meaning and the purpose of life, the whole aim and end of human existence." Thomas Jefferson later wrote that "Happiness is the aim of life, virtue is the foundation of happiness." It would appear that philosophers and historically great leaders have thought long and hard about these issues of attitude and programming ourselves towards happiness.

I once heard a National Geographic photographer speak at a seminar in Colorado and he shared that his photographic directive was always to celebrate what was right with the world! What a wonderful directive to have. Dewitt Jones has gone on to make that into a life's work for others.

Others speak of mental models or mindfulness. As we go through the course of a typical day each of us has a little voice in our heads constantly talking to us.   We carry on little conversations in our minds reflecting on a multitude of things.   What does that voice say? Is it programmed to respond positively or negatively? Is my response to find what is wrong with what I see, or to celebrate what is right with what I see?   As you watch or listen to your inner movie, do you pick out all the imperfections or do you enjoy the storyline?   Do you assume people around you will do the wrong thing or make a mistake or choose the wrong course, or do you give them the benefit of the doubt? Can you reprogram your mind to see the positive? I very much hope and believe the answer is yes. For some this tendency towards the negative can be more profound and may be a symptom of depression requiring clinical help.   For most however it is simply the way in which we process our world. As with many things, we become what we think. The premise is that if we continually find the good in what we see, increasingly we will be happier, our attitude will change and our sense of self will become a source of positive influence, not just to ourselves but also to others.

"

"Write it on your heart that every day is the best day of the year."

Ralph Waldo Emerson

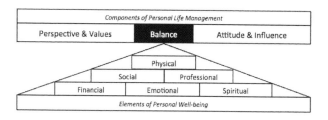

Components of Personal Life Management		
Perspective & Values	**Balance**	Attitude & Influence

		Physical		
	Social		Professional	
Financial		Emotional		Spiritual

Elements of Personal Well-being

Chapter 2: Balance

This is, perhaps the juggernaut as it relates to life fulfillment. Knowing yourself, what you are all about, what makes you tick, how you view the world and what you value most are foundational to getting to this place. Now with heightened awareness of who you are, we turn our attention to what, if anything, you are going to do differently about it. We move from theoretical concepts to more actionable items that can help you self-prescribe incremental efforts to further your own cause. For this we will explore six essential ingredients of a full and balanced life. While I am sure splitters could create other categories and others might simplify or reduce this list, it does serve as a way in which to decide how to proceed. You may emphasize or deemphasize any as you see appropriate to your own way of thinking however this authors' suggestion would be to regularly look at all six. So with that in mind, let us begin.

Elements of Personal Well-Being

1. Physical: Health and Physical Condition
2. Social: Home and Family
3. Professional: Life's Work or Career
4. Financial: Retirement or Income Goals
5. Emotional: Mental and Personal Growth
6. Spiritual: Self Fulfillment or Spirituality

Physical Well Being:
Health and Physical Condition

Do you take care of yourself? Do you see the dentist when you should, get checkups and follow preventive screening guidelines for wellness? Do you exercise, eat properly, avoid excess alcohol and all tobacco products? Are you overweight? Being the best you dictates that you address issues such as these. There are many books and web sites and products directed at personal well being. The issue is not whether the information is available, but whether or not you take and prioritize the time to take care of yourself. Exercise does not mean wearing spandex, and joining a gym membership. Walking 150 minutes a week should be within most people's grasp and gives the maximum return relating to cardiovascular fitness. Couple 75 of those minutes with vigorous activity and you are 80% there. Dental wellness including regular brushing and flossing is also associated with better cardiovascular health. Whether associated or causative is uncertain but the linkage is there. Stress reduction is something that is doable if we choose to do it. For example, yoga, meditation, Tai Chi and physical activity are all ways in which to rise above the stresses of daily life. I suspect none of this is new and it may sound pretentious, but many of the lessons of this book are simply to remind yourself to do what you already know you should. By shining a light on them and providing a systematic process of consideration we begin to lay a roadmap that is within your grasp rather than idealistic. Don't try to boil the ocean, be selective and practical and get some wins.

Social Well Being:
Home and Family

Tending to relationships is essential to a balanced life. Even individuals with strong introverted personality types, who may prefer to be alone, need personal relationships in order to thrive. In recent years a number of wilderness survival shows have appeared on popular television. In wilderness survival they speak of the rule of threes. It is said you can survive 3 minutes without air, 3 hours without shelter, 3 days without water, 3 weeks without food, and 3 months without social engagement! An increasingly popular television show called "Alone" aired in 2015 and showed 10 survival experts entering the wilderness with certain selected supplies and equipment. The person who could stay the longest would win half a million dollars! As the days and weeks progressed many solved the issues of shelter, and water and food but suffered the woes of social isolation. This became the key ingredient for many and reinforced this rule of three concept. Yes social engagement as a critical element of long-term wilderness survival. Extreme isolation draws the psyche into dark recesses and can be the difference between survival and not! So what is your social structure? Who are your friends? Are your friendships wide and shallow or narrow and deep? What about your family relationships? Do you take time for those things? Can you?

A reinforcing moment in my life was when my own father passed away. He lived about 4 hours from our own home. My family and I were there and we tended to many of the funeral arrangements and details of mourning. Family came to the wake and things were as you might expect. And yet, there we were sitting in the funeral home, at the wake, when I heard a voice. Turning I saw one of my best friends standing next to me. He and his wife chose to pick up, drive clean across the state of Florida to attend the funeral of a man they had never met. Why you might ask, because that is what friends do! I remember that day a decade ago as though it were yesterday. That relationship will stand for my lifetime and I have and will continue to be there for him as well. People may not always remember what you did for them but they will always remember the way you make them feel. I felt proud and humble and grateful and thankful for my friend and that made all the difference.

A second life story comes to mind as it relates to family. When my children were born I made it a practice to always have dinner as a family at the dinner table. As a resident physician my days and nights were consumed with long work hours away from home living and periodically sleeping at the hospital. Through all of that I stayed true to my self-imposed expectation. At times it meant coming home, having dinner, and turning around to head back to work. At other times it meant putting down the computer or the papers and protecting family time until after the children were asleep. My wife and I just celebrated our 31-year wedding anniversary. My children are grown, are college graduates, are well adjusted and have no substance abuse, legal, or other issues. I have been blessed with wonderful children and a wonderful wife. Did that family time make a difference – I like to think so. In terms of my own values and beliefs, you cannot selectively schedule quality time with your family, you can only spend time with them and from that all else will follow.

Find your own examples. Consider what matters in your social structure and material relationships. Tend to them as you would a garden. Develop a discipline around this and it, like the growth of a garden, it will yield results.

Professional Well-Being: Life's Work or Career

So where do you want to be professionally in your career? What additional training, skills or experience do you need to get there? In addition to climbing ladders, when is enough, enough and where does retirement begin to enter the picture? These are important considerations in terms of your personal career management. Without a destination it becomes impossible to chart a course and instead you simply wander aimlessly reacting to whatever winds present themselves. However, with a destination in mind, you can begin to chart a course, plot the waypoints, measure your progress and celebrate your arrival. While this is the essential first step, it should be pointed out that we are increasingly seeing individuals make wholesale career changes as adults. And so, just because you picked a destination does not mean that you cannot change your mind along the way – in fact just the opposite. As more and more information and life experience present itself, and as you clarify your own interests and objectives, you may find yourself with ever-clearer expectations around your career goals that better enable you to make difficult decisions.

Practically speaking, there are no less than three considerations to be pondered in your career deliberations. Ideally you should have a passion around your work, you should have the capacity to be good at the work, and you should be able to earn a living at the work; missing any of these three elements will likely lead to discourse in your professional well-being. For example if you are passionate and good at your work, but cannot earn a living, you will have financial worries. On the other hand if you earn big money but have no passion for your work, you may find yourself professionally frustrated or even bored or angry. Some of you are likely" saying, that is a problem I would like to have" and clearly if you filled your war chest with the spoils such that you could later explore other areas of your life, this might be a reasonable plan. For others, the doldrums of an unstimulating career become the norm with no exit plan. Selecting which wall against which to lean your ladder is important such that you don't wake up one day having summited the wall, only to be professionally frustrated in realizing it was the wrong wall.

At one point in my own career I was considering a role as the CEO of a regional health system. It meant having to relocate my family and disrupt long-standing relationships. It was clearly a professional 'next step' for me including more authority, more income, and greater prestige. I ran the idea past a good friend of mine who asked me "do you really want the job, or do you just want it because you think you can get it?" Hmmm, did I really want to be a

CEO or was that just a cultural thing that I should constantly be seeking the next big thing? We talked through what it meant and how that impacted my own personal goals. I discussed it with my wife and daughters, and my own boss and CEO at the time. At the end of the day, I withdrew from the process as it became apparent that it was not what I wanted. I was being swept away with the ideals of the position but the realities were different. Long grueling hours, on the road, outwardly facing work with politicians, local employers and dignitaries and lots of dinners and social events away from the family, were all incongruent with where I saw myself. It would have been easy to put my ladder against that wall and start climbing only later to find I had summited the wrong wall. As it turned out, the CEO position was given to an internal candidate anyway, yet I learned a valuable lesson about myself in the process.

Once you have your career destination in mind, what will it take to excel and get to where you ideally want to be? Do you need further education, experience, mentorship, resume building, exposure, or coaching? What deliberate steps can you take to get you to your goal, and on what time line are you going to accomplish those things? Committing this to paper and holding yourself accountable are key ingredients throughout this book that will help you realize your potential and your self-determined goals.

Because it is such a high area of confusion and abuse, let me make a few more observations about professional wellbeing and personal life balance before moving on. To be sure, career management and job satisfaction are clearly elements of a balanced life and are often the source of imbalance. However the concept of balance should not imply equal efforts to all things at all times. There will be periods in your life in which certain components will overshadow others. If you are in college, your studies will supersede a number of other elements. Likewise, if you start a new job that will likely take precedence. As we look at professional well-being we recognize that to balance your life in total will likely mean an overemphasis in this area for some periods of your life in order to reap those advantages at other times in your life. It is having the wherewithal to manage this element and put it in context with the other areas that are most valuable. So with that preamble, the concept of professional well being relates to identifying what you want out of your career. If you choose to be defined by your career, we simply mean to say you should do so on purpose and not feel a victim of your own doings. Conversely, if you choose not to be defined by your career, but certainly want to be professionally engaged, respected and successful, so too should that be a choice.

Financial Well-Being:
Income and Retirement Goals

Working hard and working smart are perhaps different things. Accountants have told me countless stories in which individuals worked entire careers only to struggle in retirement having never made the proper plans. I have often been amazed to learn of certain celebrities who reportedly died penniless. Judy Garland was said to be millions in debt when she died. Similarly Edgar Allen Poe, Sammy Davis Junior and Lou Costello were all said to be in debt when they passed away. Whether or not the tabloids are correct, it does underscore the reality that we each need to plan for our financial well being. Have you explored income targets, planned for college tuition(s), wedding(s), purchasing a house, a car, travel, charitable contributions or other expenditures? Do you have the proper insurance to protect yourself and your family? Depending where you are in your professional development will determine the relevance of many of these questions. There are online calculators and aids to do some of this yourself. There are also certified financial planners who will assist you in putting together a plan that works for you. If you don't have a financial plan, you should! The days of drawing a pension or social security as your vehicle of retirement are behind us. Employers are moving the decisions to their employees often with defined contribution plans in which you have to become involved in your own financial planning decisions. If you are self-employed, these are even more relevant considerations.

Emotional Well-Being:
Personal and Mental Growth

In considering the elements of a balanced life, just as we discussed in your physical well being, we need to explore your own emotional well-being. What are you doing to keep yourself intellectually challenged and emotionally growing beyond what you might do around your career or with friends and family? Each of us has interests beyond just our work, and so the question begs, do we indulge those interests? There are numerous ways in which to do this including adult courses often given by local colleges, hobbyist groups and others. There are societies, special interest groups, clubs, books, videos, web based activities, travel, and countless ways in which to learn new things or keep ourselves intellectually stimulated. Budgeting time and prioritizing your activities can make these things happen. If you are interested in photography, perhaps you take a course, or read on the subject. There is hardly a topic that you might select that resources are not available to help you develop your own understanding. In his book "How to Retire Happy, Wild and Free" Ernie Zelinski tells us to plan and create a purpose for ourselves in retirement. Too many people retire FROM their current roles, rather than TO their new role in retirement. You don't have to wait to begin indulging your own interests and personal development. Why wait for a mid-life crisis, or an end of career anniversary?

These self-indulgences don't have to be expensive. For example, I like to read. Used books are inexpensive as is book sharing with friends and neighbors. Many books are available on line at no cost at all. One of my own vehicles of personal growth relates to reading. Long ago I committed to read no less than 10 books a year. I have and usually far exceeded this self-commitment over the years. Of course now I have a study full of hundreds of books but what a wonderful problem to have.

So develop yourself and be the multifaceted, complex person you want to be. Don't wait until it is too late. The old phrase that "I never met someone who on their death bed wished they had worked harder" seems to fit. Make your life deliberate, make it stimulating, and make it what you want it to be!

Spiritual Well-Being:
Self Fulfillment or Spirituality

Self-fulfillment and spiritual well being is not intended to mean religion. While for many this may be the vehicle, here we define the term more broadly. Fellowship and service to others, meditation, Feng Shui (Chinese art of placement), Tai Chi and Japanese Reiki (universal life force energy) in addition to prayer, ministry and religious studies are all ways in which to address your own sense of self-fulfillment or spiritual well-being. For some it is escaping into the woods to spend time alone with themselves in the splendor of the outdoors, for others it is weekly attendance at church. For others, such as the Patron Saint Francis of the Roman Catholic Church, it is both. St Francis was a 12th Century Italian and Roman Catholic Friar who later became the patron saint of ecology and the environment. He walked among the animals and nature and found solace and happiness in it. Today he is often seen as a statute in birdbaths surrounded by animals.

Each of these examples are how others found spirituality in their lives. Consider your own values and what brings a sense of self-fulfillment and spiritual well being to you and make it a conscious effort. Finding inner peace and knowing how to recharge are essential components of leading a balanced life. In the movie "The Bucket List" Morgan Freeman, playing Carter, a man dying of cancer, speaks of the spiritual nature and majesty of his mountains. You can feel the energy as he ponders the mountains' splendor, perhaps the way the Polynesian culture feels "mana" or the power of energy and spirit. Whatever your vehicle, your culture, your history, your experiences or your personal beliefs, find a way to explore it, practice it and make it a part of your routine.

Elements of Personal Excellence

1. Perspective and Attitude

2. Balance (Six Components)

3. Values

4. Influence

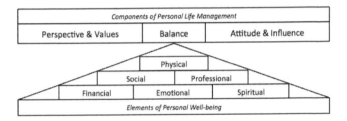

Without goals, who knows where we will end up?

"

"Your beliefs become your thoughts,
Your thoughts become your words,
Your words become your actions,
Your actions become your habits,
Your habits become your values,
Your values become your destiny."

Mahatma Gandhi

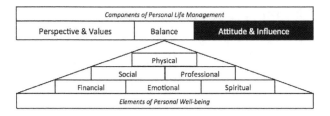

Components of Personal Life Management		
Perspective & Values	Balance	Attitude & Influence

		Physical		
	Social		Professional	
Financial		Emotional		Spiritual

Elements of Personal Well-being

Chapter 3: Values

What do you value most? Have you ever thought about it? Here is an interesting exercise to help sort it out. Imagine your house is on fire and you have but a few moments to react. What would you do? Can you write that down and prioritize it from one to ten? We have done this exercise countless times with groups of participants with just those instructions. Did you list people on your list? If not, did you take that for granted? Is that symbolic of how you treat your loved ones? Of the material possessions, what did you list? The first time I did this exercise I came to the realization that after my family, the only thing I valued was my memories. My photographs were the most important memory aid to me followed closely by my personal journals. I live in Florida where hurricanes are a real threat and have had to be on alert to evacuate my home on numerous occasions. In the early phases my wife and I would pack the house up. We would have cartons of things to fill our station wagon or van, and were always at the ready to evacuate. After this personal value exercise we came to the realization that the home was replaceable but the people and many of the photographs were not. We scanned our old photographs to a digital drive and keep two backups. Today, in the event of a fire or hurricane, all we do today is get the family out and take at least one hard-drive copy of our lifetime pictures. It was a refreshing exercise that was sobering and liberating at the same time; especially for someone like me who likes to collect things! So what is most precious to you, what are your personal values?

Another way to clarify values is to write a personal mission statement. This technique is used by industries all around the world. It is an exercise, that when done well, should commit to writing what you are all about. What is your purpose in life, what brings you happiness, how do you want to spend your time, how do you measure personal success? Answers to questions such as these can be helpful in prioritizing what you do and allow you to effectively manage your time, your resources and ultimately your life.

"

"To leave the world a bit better, whether by a healthy child, a garden patch or a redeemed social condition; to know that even one life has breathed easier because you lived- that is to have succeeded."

Ralph Waldo Emerson

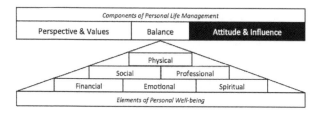

Components of Personal Life Management		
Perspective & Values	Balance	**Attitude & Influence**

Physical

Social | Professional

Financial | Emotional | Spiritual

Elements of Personal Well-being

Chapter 4: Influence

In the movie entitled "The Bucket List" starring Jack Nicholson and Morgan Freeman, there is a scene atop a great pyramid in which Mr. Freeman's character speaks of the ancient Egyptians and their belief that souls approaching the entrance to heaven were asked two questions. Their answers to those questions determined whether or not they were able to enter. The first question asked is "have you found joy in your life?" This is a question worth considering yourself and is the essence of this entire writing. The second question however rides hand in hand with the first and asks, "has your life brought joy to others?" What influence have you had upon those about you? Tom Stevenin was a wonderful author, businessman, lecturer, and educator who spoke of the concept of being a center of positive influence for others. Do you bring joy to others? Are you a center of positive influence? Do you believe this matter? There are many quotes and signs based around this topic; "To give is to receive", etc. Many authors who have studied this space would argue that bringing joy and happiness to others in fact does help us self-actualize and be happier. This socialized function of interacting with others in positive and productive ways in some fashion must be deeply rooted with our need to be with people in general. Remember the rule of threes and the need to socialize. Here we suggest that this socialization is best if positive. Perhaps reprogramming our minds to see the good in people, to see what is right in our world, to find what is virtuous and to increasingly live in that space will translate to happier more joyful life overall.

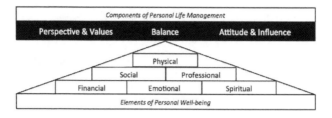

Components of Personal Life Management

| Perspective & Values | Balance | Attitude & Influence |

Physical
Social | Professional
Financial | Emotional | Spiritual

Elements of Personal Well-being

Chapter 5: Putting it all together

As with many readings, it is easy to read these pages, potentially agree with the ideas and concepts and simply fall back into your old way of doing things. We all have our own styles and attributes that make us the unique set of people we are. Knowing yourself, including your style, your tendencies, your positive and negative tendencies, let me suggest some ways in which to use the teachings of this short guide as a vehicle of personal change and life management.

First, consider where you are in your own life's journey and how balanced and happy you consider yourself to be. If you saw no room for improvement chances are you would not have been reading this to begin with. And so I would suggest you take some time to ponder the teachings and come back to them. If you are a list maker, perhaps you can begin with the exercises, which have been reproduced in the appendix of this writing. If you are less of a reader or a list maker than let me suggest that you select one to two things that you intend to do differently as a result of reading this book and that you share that with a trusted friend or family member. The act of discussing it with someone else will solidify your commitment to the change and will make it tangible – a type of assisted personal accountability. Instead of a one-time New Year's resolution, it will become something you tend to. I personally keep a daily journal and find this helpful when I reflect upon the years' activities. Since I handle the on a near daily basis I put my goals in the back cover of the diary; it makes it easy to find and easy to keep front and center in my thinking's.

Second, we have purposefully kept this writing condensed and practical in order to encourage you to return to the materials over and over. Some of the best readings that have impacted my life are things I have re-read countless times over decades of life experiences. As you evolve over time you may glean or find value in different components of this work. Write in the margins, take notes, make it a workbook of life and not an epitaph of should-have-dones.

Finally, the notion of personal resiliency is a hot topic in the literature. It is the sum total measure of our personal strength and ability to tolerate unpleasant happenings in our life. If you are strong in some areas, perhaps you can absorb challenges better in other areas. Hence the idea of personal resiliency is not to be looked at in isolation. Building upon your areas of strength will give you a starting point from which to build. Revel in your strengths as you identify areas in which to develop. Celebrate something every day; make it a part of your being.

Closing

This writing reflects my own life experiences over the last half-century. I have gleaned thoughts and ideas from many sources and have stood on the shoulders of great leaders, educators, theologians, and people in general. While I do not claim to be an expert in any of these skills I do believe that life is about the journey and not just the final destination. I believe that how we live our lives matters. I do not believe that any of us want to be miserable, or thought poorly of, or angry, or sad, or unfulfilled. Instead I choose to believe that people are basically good and want to be happy, fulfilled, and joyful. I welcome the thoughts and ideas of others as we look for ways in which to achieve that state of personal wellbeing.

About the Author

Bruce Flareau and his wife Kathy have two grown daughters, Danielle and Christine, are longtime residents of Tampa bay Florida. As a practicing family physician, and professor in two universities, Bruce was a recognized academic scholar writing articles and textbook chapters while teaching countless residents and medical students over the years. He later went on to become a physician executive with system responsibility across a large integrated delivery system. He has authored books on topics such as population health and on physician leadership. Through all of his professional successes however Dr. Flareau never lost sight of the other elements of his life. An outdoors enthusiast, he and his family have traveled the globe including Antarctica, Africa, the Arctic Circle, Alaska and other extreme environments photographing polar bears, humpback whales and hosts of other scenic environments and wild animals in their natural surroundings. In addition to amateur wildlife and nature photographer he is accomplished boat captain, fisherman, and SCUBA diver, not to mention backwoodsman. At home he enjoys woodworking, reading and writing and spending time with the family.

Appendix: Exercise Worksheets

Activity #1
Eulogy Exercise

Imagine that you have just arrived at a funeral and you walk up to the front of the room, gaze into the casket and suddenly come face to face with yourself. This is your funeral, 3 years from today. As you calmly sit down and review the program, you see that there are to be four speakers.

The first is from your family; this might be a brother, sister, aunt, uncle or some other family member who knew you well. The second is a personal friend, someone who can speak of you as a person. The third is a professional colleague, and the fourth is from your church or a community organization that you worked with.

Think deeply as to what you would want each of these people to say about you.

What kind of husband, wife, father, or mother would you want their words to reflect? What kind of son, or daughter, or friend, or professional colleague would you want them to have seen you as? What character would you want them to have seen in you? What contributions or achievements would you wish to be remembered for? What differences would you like to have made in the lives of the people around you?

Take a few moments and write down your reflections to these questions.

Colleague

_____

_____

_____

_____

_____

_____

_____

_____

_____

_____

_____

_____

Family

_____

_____

_____

_____

_____

_____

_____

_____

_____

_____

_____

Friend

_____

_____

_____

_____

_____

_____

_____

_____

_____

_____

_____

_____

Community and Church

_____

_____

_____

_____

_____

_____

_____

_____

_____

Character

_____

_____

_____

_____

_____

_____

_____

_____

_____

_____

_____

_____

Achievement or Contribution

_____

_____

_____

_____

_____

_____

_____

_____

_____

_____

_____

_____

What would you want your headstone to read?

Hear lies

_____,

She/ he was ….

_____

_____

_____

_____

_____

_____

_____

_____

_____

_____

_____

_____

_____

_____

_____

Activity #2
Values and Mission

What do I value most? If my house was on fire and I could save only five things, <u>what would I choose</u>? And why?

Rank from highest to lowest priority

1.

_____

_____

_____

_____

_____

_____

_____

_____

_____

_____

_____

_____

2.

_____

_____

_____

_____

_____

_____

_____

_____

_____

_____

3.

_____

_____

_____

_____

_____

_____

_____

_____

_____

_____

4.

_____

_____

_____

_____

_____

_____

_____

_____

_____

_____

5.

_____

_____

_____

_____

_____

_____

_____

_____

_____

_____

Activity #3
Write your Mission Statement

Reflect on what you consider to be the greatest moments in your life?

- Is it a single event?
- A series of events?
- A theme or concept?

_____

_____

_____

_____

_____

_____

_____

_____

_____

_____

_____

_____

_____

_____

_____

Activity #4
Goal Writing Exercise

Home and Family Goals: (time allocation, activities, recreation, family, friends, time with spouse, children)

_____
_____
_____
_____
_____
_____
_____
_____
_____
_____

Professional Goals: (practice type, location, academics, second careers)

_____
_____
_____
_____
_____
_____

_____

_____

_____

_____

_____

_____

_____

_____

Financial Goals: (income needs,
retirement, income, long term and short
term income, insurance, contributions
to church and community)

_____

_____

_____

_____

_____

_____

_____

_____

_____

_____

_____

_____

Training and Personal Development Goals: (Courses, books, CD/DVD, travel, growth experiences)

_____

_____

_____

_____

_____

_____

_____

_____

_____

_____

_____

Spiritual Goals: (fellowship, service to others, meditation, prayer, study ministry)

_____

_____

_____

_____

_____

_____

_____

_____

_____

_____

_____

_____

_____

Health and Physical Well-Being Goals:
(weight, exercise, relaxation, nutrition,
health screening, stress management)

_____

_____

_____

_____

_____

_____

_____

_____

_____

_____

_____

_____

_____

_____

_____

Activity #5
Positive Psychology

God grant me the serenity to accept the things I cannot change; the courage to change the things I can; and the wisdom to know the difference

-American theologian Reinhold Niebuhr

What will your verse be?

_____

_____

_____

_____

_____

_____

_____

_____

_____

_____

_____

_____

_____

What two goals do I want to work on in the next 6 to 12 months?

1.

_____

_____

_____

_____

_____

_____

_____

_____

_____

2.

_____

_____

_____

_____

_____

_____

_____

_____

_____

Activity #6
Positive Influence
Being a Center of Positive Influence
(*Bringing Joy to Others*)

CONSIDERATIONS

- Is bringing joy to others a necessary step in attaining personal happiness?
- Is being a center of positive influence a worthwhile endeavor towards personal happiness? (pay-it-forward concept)

INDIVIDUAL ACTIVITY

Do I bring joy into my daily activities with others?

_____

_____

_____

_____

_____

_____

_____

_____

Am I a center of positive influence for others? If so, who?

_____

_____

_____

_____

_____

_____

_____

_____

_____

_____

_____

_____

_____

_____

_____

_____

_____

_____

_____

_____

Activity #7
What Makes You Happy?

Activities (the things you "do")

_____

_____

_____

_____

_____

_____

_____

_____

_____

_____

_____

_____

_____

_____

_____

_____

_____

_____

_____

_____

People

Places

Events or Situations

_____

_____

_____

_____

_____

_____

_____

_____

_____

_____

_____

_____

_____

_____

_____

_____

_____

_____

_____

_____

_____

_____

_____

_____

Additional Resources to Guide You Further on Your Journey

Buford, Bob. *Halftime: moving from success to significance.* Grand Rapids, MI: Sondervan, 2008. Print.

Canfield, Jack and Mark Victor. Hansen. *Chicken soup for the soul: 101 stories to open the heart & rekindle the spirit.* Deerfield Beach, FL: Health Communications, 1993. Print.

Carison, Richard. *Don't sweat the small stuff—and it's all small stuff: simple ways to keep the little things from taking over your life.* New York: Hyperion, 1997. Print.

Collins, James C. *Good to great: why some companies make the leap… and others don't.* New York, NY: HarperBusiness. 2001. Print.

Covey, Stephen R. The 7 habits o f highly
effective people: powerful
lessons in personal change. New
York: Simon & Shuster, 2013.
Print.

Dewitt Jones; Celebrate what is right
with the world:
http://dewittjones.com/celebrate
.htm

Kushner, Harold S. *Living a life that
matters: resolving the conflict
between conscience and success.*
New York: A.A. Knopf, 2001. Print.

Positive Psychology:
www.positivepsychology.org/

Zelinski, Ernie J. *How to retire happy,
wild and free: retirement wisdom
that you wont get from your
financial advisor.* Berkeley, CA:
Ten Speed Press, 2004. Print.

Reader Notes:

_____

_____

_____

_____

_____

_____

_____

_____

_____

_____

_____

_____

_____

_____

_____

_____

_____

_____

_____

_____

_____

_____

_____

Reader Notes:

_____

_____

_____

_____

_____

_____

_____

_____

_____

_____

_____

_____

_____

_____

_____

_____

_____

_____

_____

_____

_____

_____

Reader Notes:

_____

_____

_____

_____

_____

_____

_____

_____

_____

_____

_____

_____

_____

_____

_____

_____

_____

_____

_____

_____

_____

_____

_____

Reader Notes:

_____
_____
_____
_____
_____
_____
_____
_____
_____
_____
_____
_____
_____
_____
_____
_____
_____
_____
_____
_____
_____

Reader Notes:

Other Works by this Author

<u>The Six P's of Physician Leadership:</u>
<u>A Primer for Emerging and Developing Leaders</u>

The Six P's of Physician Leadership is an executive and academically focused primer that identifies six essential issues for every current, up and coming, and potential physician leader that they can incorporate in their daily work and life. It brings a fresh understanding on the topics of people, presence, politics, process, perspective, and principles of business that are targeted to physician leaders but with universal application in leadership development.

The authors explore each of the P's in unequal amounts and raise your awareness of their relevance to physician leadership. Written from experience gained as a physician executive and a business strategist who has worked to understand the essence of the dilemmas and challenges faced by physicians in the transition from the cottage industry of the twentieth-century to today's evolving clinically integrated care delivery environment. The book concludes with a glimpse of additional critical issues that include governance, career management and work-life balance.

Becoming a leader and remaining a great leader is a personal journey of self-development. In the physician realm, there are minimal resources directed to their unique circumstances. With a global health care system that is rapidly evolving in the digital age more physician leaders will be required to champion organizational transformation across the global healthcare landscape. An industry level renaissance to support systemic challenges is occurring in healthcare and the need to cultivate leadership essentials has never been more important.

Available in digital and print versions

- Page Intentionally Left Blank -

Made in the USA
Lexington, KY
04 June 2018